"In a rapidly changing world, Mr. Jenkins Told Me … is a reminder that the fundamentals don't change. How people are treated, how they are managed and how they are led still determine the success and longevity of a business. This book is a great read for those interested in learning the building blocks of a business built for the long haul."

VERNE HARNISH, FOUNDER ENTREPRENEURS ORGANIZATION (EO)
AND AUTHOR OF SCALING UP (ROCKEFELLER HABITS 2.0)

"I can honestly say I *needed* the lessons in this book. Morris-Jenkins is one of the highest performing values-based businesses I've ever seen and the humility of Jonathan Bancroft is nothing short of captivating as he shares the leadership lessons he learned from that most extraordinary of mentors; *Mr. Jenkins Told Me* … is a wonderfully written tale that every business leader needs to read."

KEITH MERCURIO, DIRECTOR OF TRAINING STRATEGY, NEXSTAR NETWORK
AND MASTER TRAINER OF OVER 20,000 HOME SERVICE PROFESSIONALS

"Morris-Jenkins has grown from a small air conditioning service company to one that dominates its local market and is now one of the largest in the industry. In this book, Jonathan Bancroft tells that story in a very human way and provides enduring principles for dealing with the people side of business. Highly recommended reading for those interested in building a lasting organization."

MICHAEL GERBER, AUTHOR OF THE E-MYTH SERIES

MR. JENKINS
TOLD ME...

MR. JENKINS
TOLD
ME...

"Forgotten Principles
That Will
Grow Any Business"

JONATHAN BANCROFT
WITH ROY H WILLIAMS

ISBN 978-1-932226-22-5

Printed in the United States of America 2019

Visit *www.MrJenkinsToldMe.com*
Contact: *book@morrisjenkins.com*

Content

Acknowledgements

The stories I've shared have shaped me as a person and have molded my beliefs into what they are today. While I'm certainly not a professional writer, my wish is that you get some enjoyment in reading these stories and possibly even take some of these core concepts and apply them in your own life or business.

I want to thank Alton Powell for interviewing and hiring me on the spot all those years ago. Your decision opened a door and helped save a young man who needed an opportunity.

My journey wouldn't have gotten much further than the first couple of days if it hadn't been for Chuck Nickels agreeing to let a young know-nothing hop into his truck and then teaching him what it means to work for Dewey Jenkins. I fell in love with this trade while riding around with Chuck.

I believe there is truly an art to storytelling, and my journey wouldn't have been what it is without the tutelage of one of the greatest storytellers I've ever met, David Smith. You taught me how to transfer knowledge with enthusiasm, and spent countless hours teaching me how to tell my own stories.

This book could not have been written without the dedication and talents of Casey Welch. You have a keen sense of awareness and ability to shape and package content that people want to hear, see, and feel. I appreciate your friendship and guidance.

The wisdom and creativity of Roy H. Williams is truly one of the world's wonders. No other writing partner could have possibly helped get my story told. You are a wizard of words, and I'm thankful for you sharing your wisdom and creativity on this project.

I married well above my pay grade. You've heard that before, right? I want to thank my wonderful wife, Blaire, for agreeing to go with me on that first date to a Mexican restaurant and a minor league baseball game and allowing me to share some stories of what your father has told me over the years. You're my best friend and the love of my life.

I lost my mother when I was 26 years old. I gained a second mother at 28, when I got married. Reneé Jenkins made me feel as if I've been a part of the Jenkins family from the beginning. She's the matriarch of this story in many ways. Thank you for accepting me into this family and supporting all of us as we went off to fix everyone's air conditioner, and never making me feel like I was a son-in-law, but rather just a son.

Dewey Jenkins has always said that he doesn't believe people come to his doorstep by complete chance. He's made me a believer in that philosophy as well. I came to his doorstep in desperation, without knowing who he was. Through this encounter I found out what I enjoyed doing for a living and that I was talented enough to do it well. When Dewey Jenkins speaks, everyone stops to listen intently. One of those listeners just had to write a book about the things he heard him say. Thank you, Dewey, for believing in me and allowing me to share these stories.

Jonathan Bancroft

Foreword

Richard Olivier doesn't know me, but he explains why this book had to be written:

"We'll always know the numbers, the statistics, and the trends. But how often do we take time to tell the story of the past? Not the result but the process, not the 'what' but the 'why' and the 'how'? Wherever we are and whatever we do, we're all, always, part of a story. Human beings have always passed on knowledge this way; stories are storehouses of wisdom that teach and inspire us. There isn't a day goes by that we don't tell, hear, read, or see a story from children, partners, friends, or the media. But then we go to work and start reporting only facts and speaking in acronyms. A leader who doesn't know what story he or she is in, and where they are within it, is missing an essential route to inspiration."

—RICHARD OLIVIER,
INSPIRATIONAL LEADERSHIP, HENRY V AND THE MUSE OF FIRE, P. 10

Thank you, Richard. Now I know what I need to do.

—JONATHAN BANCROFT

Preface
Putting Things in Perspective

A successful local air conditioning company brings in about $5 million a year in revenues. An air conditioning company that's doing $10 million is exceptional. A $20 million company will be known and admired by air conditioning people from coast to coast. The struggling little $1 million company purchased by Mr. Jenkins is now knocking on the door of $100 million a year in Charlotte, North Carolina.

And I was there to watch it come together, piece by piece. My name is Jonathan Bancroft.

David Smith, our longtime sales manager, just celebrated his 25th anniversary with the company. Dave Hearne, our longtime installation director, is celebrating his 28th. Installers Terry Sigmon and Scott Stallings have both spent 25 years with the company. Allen Smith, our newly appointed Sales Director, has 19 years with the company, and David Dupuy, Senior Service Technician, has 18. The blood, sweat, tears, and DNA of these people and others like them are the cement that binds this company into something solid and true.

And the guiding hand that put it all together doesn't know how to fix an air conditioner. Dewey Jenkins could just as easily have purchased a broken down, broken-hearted sports team that no one loved—a team that had never won a game—and turned them into world champions.

But Mr. Jenkins wouldn't have created his championship team by studying the game, the sport itself. And he wouldn't have done it by studying his opponents, their strengths and their weaknesses. And he wouldn't have done it by recruiting superstar talent.

Mr. Jenkins would have created his world champion team by understanding his customers—the fans of the game—and then giving them exactly the experience they were hoping to have. His only question for his team would have been, "How can we make people really glad they came to see us play?" And then, when his team got excited about something to make the fans—the people buying the tickets—really happy, he would smile and say, "Okay. Let's do that, then."

Mr. Jenkins has only two questions:

1. "How can we give our customers a better experience?"
2. "What can we eliminate, or make easier, so that doing business with us is effortless, happy, and fun?"

By reframing the objective of the game, Mr. Jenkins has attracted a new kind of player and then given that player a new kind of joy. Everyone in our city wants to work at Morris-Jenkins.

Mr. Jenkins isn't a superhero, a motivational speaker, or even a rah-rah cheerleader.

He is a kind and gentle man.

I've never seen him angry.

Mr. Jenkins Told Me...

"The Place to Start is Where You Are."

I woke up with a state trooper in my bedroom. My father was dead. I was seven years old.

My dad, Philip Bancroft, was a young architect, just getting started. He was driving home from Hartsville, South Carolina, where he had been working on a project. We don't know exactly what happened, but he ran off the road. Maybe a deer leaped onto the road or something. He wasn't wearing a seatbelt. It was 1981. He was thrown out of the car.

I never really got into trouble as a kid, never got into a dark place, but I definitely had a chip on my shoulder. I convinced myself that I was the underdog. I had to teach myself how to tie a fishing knot, you know? And when everybody else's dad was watching them at the little league game, I didn't have a dad out there. My mom was doing absolutely everything she could, but I didn't really know that then like I do now. And it never occurred to me that millions of other kids were growing up in circumstances exactly like my own.

I grew up with a chip on my shoulder, but that chip didn't turn me into a bully. It drove me, pushed me to overcome my disadvantages. I was unwilling to quit, unwilling to lose, unwilling to feel sorry for myself. The bottled-up anger I felt about the loss of my dad expressed itself as drive and determination. But no matter how hard I worked, I couldn't make enough money to put myself through college. Things went from bad to worse. I was desperate.

That's when Mom called to ask how I was doing. After a few minutes, she said, "I was hoping you could join us for Sunday dinner." I thought, "Great! After we've washed the dishes, I'll talk to Mom because I'm in bad trouble here. I'm thousands of dollars in debt." I was 23 years old and buried in credit card obligations, trying to fund an education.

She didn't tell me there were going to be other people at dinner. I didn't know any of them, but one lady kept talking about this place called Morris-Jenkins where her husband worked. She said they were looking to hire some folks with good communication skills who wanted to learn a trade.

She said, "Morris-Jenkins teaches people from the ground up and gives them a real career. And they don't charge a penny for it. In fact, they pay you while you're learning." That was the first I had ever heard of Morris-Jenkins. I had no idea that my life was about to change forever.

It took me awhile to figure out that my mom's friend was hinting that I ought to consider applying for a job at Morris-Jenkins. So after dinner I circled back and said, "Mom, I'd like to talk to those people." She smiled and gave me a phone number and told me to ask for the service manager, Alton Powell.

I called Alton, and he invited me to come over and talk. This was the winter of 1998, just before Christmas. It was the first time I had ever been in a professional interview. He was very matter-of-fact, listened to my story, and hired me at the end of it. I remember him saying, "Jonathan, it's going to be monkey-see, monkey-do. You're either going to love it, or it's not going to be for you. And if it's not for you, that's okay. We'll wish you well and support you all the way."

That was my first glimpse of the kindness at the core of this big-hearted company. I've watched the team at Morris-Jenkins invest in people, try to help people, and get nothing in return for their investment. But no matter what, they're always on your side. They want the best for you, whatever that might be.

Alton suggested that I sit in on an after-hours training class with the 14 technicians who already worked there. I didn't know what they were talking about, but I looked around that room and said to myself, "There are 14 men in this room, and they all seem like really nice guys. They obviously know what this instructor's talking about, so dang it, if they can do this, so can I."

My first day was January 11th, 1999. It had been a bitterly cold weekend, so when they took me to the service manager's office, it was just frantic. It looked like a news room from the 1960s. Complete pandemonium. I was new to this, so it didn't occur to me that the phones were going crazy because of the weather. Alton told me that he was going to be right with me, but he had some things he had to take care of first.

He said there was a desk in the warehouse and that if I'd grab a seat there, he'd be with me as soon as he could. Nobody knows me, and I don't know them. But on the desk is this monster catalog from Grainger Supply. It's as big as a Sears catalogue from the 1970s, times ten. I mean, it was huge. I started thumbing through it.

Ten o'clock comes and goes.

Eleven o'clock comes and goes.

Noon comes and goes. One o'clock, two o'clock, three o'clock, four o'clock. The whole day goes by, and I wasn't assertive enough to walk back in there and say, "Hey, yoo-hoo, you forgot about me!"

Five o'clock comes, and I drive home a little depressed. "Do I come back for day two? Do they even need me? I don't know what's going on."

I came back for day two, and it was still a beehive of activity. Alton was *sooooo* sorry for leaving me in that situation, and after he explained how busy they were yesterday, I sort of understood. So now I'm sitting around waiting for him again.

5

After about an hour, I saw what looked to be an old veteran technician headed across the warehouse toward a truck parked outside the bay door. He had two or three boxes under each arm, an unlit cigarette bobbing at the corner of his mouth, and his baseball cap was on backwards and cocked to one side. I said, "This guy's been a tech for a long time, and I'm not sitting here at this desk for another eight hours." So I popped up, shot across the warehouse floor, grabbed the boxes from under one of his arms and said, "I'm Jonathan, the new guy."

He straightened his hat, looked down at my shoe tips, then up to my face. "Well, my name's Chuck. If you wanna ride with me, come on." For the next two weeks I rode with Chuck every day. We were on an adventure! I was fixing units and doing other stuff I had no clue how to do, but Chuck was teaching, and I was learning.

That's when I knew this was going to be my career. Riding with Chuck, I fell in love with heating and air conditioning. Driving down the road, I'd always be smiling because, "Dang it man, I'm good at this!"

And to make it even better, I had found a dependable way to get out of debt.

Jonathan around age 7

Jonathan and his Mom playing in woods behind their home in Camden, SC

2

Mr. Jenkins Told Me...

"Listen to People Who are Wiser and Smarter than You."

C huck said Mr. Jenkins called the whole company together for a Saturday meeting a few years earlier because a guy named Jim Rohn told him, "If you're going to be successful, you've got to find your true north, because the storms are going to batter you and spin you around in different directions if you don't have values and commitments that tell you which way to go."

This idea of finding your true north and letting it be your guiding light has been around since Henry David Thoreau wrote *Walden* in 1854. He said we should, "Be as the sailor who keeps the polestar in his eye. By doing so we will maintain a true course."

But the real key, I think, is to be able to look into the star-filled heavens and pick the one star that will be your guiding light. For Morris-Jenkins, it was this: "Above all else, respect our customers. Respect their time, respect their money, respect how they want to be served."

Chuck continued his story, "Mr. Jenkins gathered everyone together to talk and agree on the values and commitments that would become this company's guiding light. At the end of that day, everyone said, 'This is what we believe. This is who we are.' I wasn't there, but I'm told it was a real good exercise and everyone went home with a good feelin' but most of those people didn't understand that Mr. Jenkins wasn't just playin.' He was really gonna do this stuff."

Chuck looked over at me to see if I was listening. I nodded my head quickly up and down, so he continued. "Back then, air conditioning companies worked Monday through Friday from 8:00 till 4:00 or 4:30. And when quittin' time came, we'd just go home. Wouldn't matter if a customer had air conditioning or not. We'd just leave. But Mr. Jenkins said that was gonna change. From here on out, Morris-Jenkins was gonna take care of its customers, no matter what."

Chuck chuckled, low and raspy. "He even got his wife and daughters to write a little jingle and put it on TV." Then he cleared his throat and began singing, "Late last night I woke up sweating in my bed. That old air conditioner, it was completely dead. So I called Morris-Jenkins and they very kindly said, 'You'll have cool air at your house tonight!'"

Then Chuck slowly began turning his head from side-to-side. "Lost every technician he had. Quit. Every one of 'em. All he had left was one technician-in-training, a fella that used to be his warehouse man. Turns out that values and commitments are a lot of fun 'til you have to start livin' up to 'em. But Mr. Jenkins didn't back off. Lost money every month for a year 'til he had put together a crew of technicians that were willin' to stay on the job 'til it was done."

"Was that when you came to work here, Chuck?"

Chuck nodded his head, "Shortly thereafter." And then he wrapped it up. "By not backing off, Mr. Jenkins set a new standard and everybody hired after that understood that if you want to work at Morris-Jenkins, here's what you're gonna do. And that," concluded Chuck, "was that."

Mr. Jenkins and employees posing for photo after the Saturday meeting to establish company Values & Commitments

Mr. Jenkins Told Me...

"The Time to Start is Now."

I had moved into the basement of my mom's house and was crawling out of debt. But one of my goals was to save up enough money to buy a copy of *Modern Refrigeration and Air Conditioning*, the Bible of air conditioning.

Finally, the big day came. I walked into a Borders bookstore and bought it.

Each night when I got back to my basement, I'd pore through that book trying to become the best technician in the company. Finally, they gave me an old Dodge Dakota, one of those little mid-sized trucks, and sent me out to fly solo. That old Dodge shook and rattled, and I smelled like cigar smoke every time I stepped out of it, even though I didn't smoke. I scrubbed it with everything I could find, but that cigar smell was baked into the soul of that little truck.

I spent the next year and a half as a maintenance technician, cleaning units, which was not what I was hoping to do. But when it was really hot or really cold and all the other guys wanted to go home to their families, I would call in to dispatch and say, "Hey, I'm sure there's some 'no heat' calls or some 'no air conditioning' calls on the board. Throw them my way, and I won't quit until those units are working."

I think that might have been when Mr. Jenkins first noticed me.

Our new service manager was getting ready to start his weekly meeting when Alton showed up at the meeting room door. He looked at me, and I looked at him, and he crooked his finger like, "Come here."

I thought, "Uh-oh, am I in trouble?"

I walked over, and he said, "I want to talk to you. Let's go to breakfast." On the way to the diner, he said they wanted to offer me a sales job. I didn't have to interview for it; they'd seen enough.

I was stunned. This wasn't even on my radar.

I joyfully took the job but then had a difficult 12 months during my first year in sales. This might have been because shortly after I got the job, I learned my mom had terminal cancer. But whatever the reason, I felt I was getting all the really tough sales leads. I mentioned this to one of the other salesmen, and he said, "Really? You're getting the tough sales leads? You ought to talk to Mr. Jenkins about that."

I asked, "Are you sure?"

He said, "Oh yeah, Mr. Jenkins would want to hear about that. He can definitely give you some help with that."

So I said, "Okay, I'm going to go in there and tell Mr. Jenkins about these leads."

That's when I learned that Mr. Jenkins is the world's greatest listener. I'd had a hard year in sales, and I was venting to him. He listened with interest and then shared some words of wisdom with me and encouraged me a little. Then he told me exactly how much money it took to generate each of those leads. He said, "These leads are precious. We have everything invested in these leads, and the whole company is counting on you to do your best on every sales call."

Then, just as I was walking out, he said, "Jonathan."

I turned around to see Mr. Jenkins standing up, smiling his most encouraging smile. "Problems are here to strengthen us. You learn how to overcome a problem, and it will never be a problem again."

That's the last time I ever went into Mr. Jenkins' office to complain about the sales leads I was getting.

The other sales guys were laughing at me when I walked back into the sales office.

But I had decided to start doing the things Mr. Jenkins had told me during the past 12 months. He'd said, "Listen to people who are wiser and smarter than you." And he'd said, "The job of a leader is to search the world for the best advice, and then bring it back to your organization and your family."

So I figured I should start doing those things.

Ray Isaac is a friend of Mr. Jenkins who owns Isaac Heating in Rochester, New York. He has a house on the waterfront with a 100-foot cliff at the edge of his yard where the waves come crashing up from Lake Ontario.

Ray invited me up to his place to play golf and go boating with some other guys we both know.

But I didn't make that trip to go boating or to play golf. I went to see Ray because he's smarter and wiser than me. I went to see Ray so that I could bring back his sage advice to my company and my family.

I was looking up from the water at Ray's house on the cliff when I asked him, "What's the secret of your success, Ray?"

That's when I got what I came for. Ray said, "It's a formula called The Six E's. Engage, Educate, Empower, and Enable. And you've got to do it in exactly that order."

"Engage, educate, empower, and enable?"

Ray nodded yes. Then he said,

"1. **Engage** people with an attitude of servitude. Your job is to make things better for them.

2. **Educate** the people you depend on. Don't expect them to already know what to do.

3. Empower them to make a decision, and if they make a bad decision, go back to educate. But continue to empower them.

4. Enable people to do what they do best."

"But you said there were Six E's."

Ray nodded again. "After the fourth E, there's an equals sign. And on the other side of that equals sign is **5. Execute.** You see, you've got to actually execute your plan to engage, educate, empower, and enable. And then comes the sixth E."

"What's that?"

"**6. Enjoy.** You get to enjoy what you do. But Jonathan, there's also an evil E."

I raised my eyebrows. "Evil?"

Ray nodded one more time. "Yes, evil. The evil E is always there. It surrounds you, and it tries to carve itself into your bones. And if it can do that, it will destroy you."

Flying home from Ray's place, I realized that I had been feeling entitled to sell to people who already understood why air conditioning costs so much and who weren't suspicious of salesmen. And even before I got into sales, I had been feeling entitled to make service calls all day instead of cleaning the outside coils for countless monthly maintenance customers.

I've been guarding against **Entitlement** ever since.

4

Mr. Jenkins Told Me...

"No One is Born a Diamond."

When\ I got back from my visit with Ray Isaacs, Mr. Jenkins told me I was getting a brand-new truck. I figured it would be another plain Jane little Dodge Dakota, but at least this one wouldn't smell like cigar smoke.

But boy, was I wrong. It was a brand-new Chevrolet Silverado, Extended Cab LT with power everything. I definitely didn't feel entitled to it.

My mom was very weak by then, but I remember driving that truck over to show it to her. She had given her whole life to raising my little brother and me, and I needed her to see that her love and devotion and sacrifice had put my brother and me on a good track. I knew the only way to make her happy was to let her see my brother and me happy, so I told her how well I was doing and how I owed it all to her. She could barely come outside, but she made it, and I could tell that she was deeply satisfied to see that I was finally on my way.

We lost her a few months later. My brother and I were now alone.

I was adrift.

The sun came up, and I went to work. The sun went down, and I went home.

The sun came up, and I went to work. The sun went down, and I went home.

The sun came up, and I went to work. The sun went down, and I went home.

I don't know how long this went on, but I do know that I wasn't completely there.

Then one day I came into the office, and there was plastic on the floor and painter's tape everywhere. I said, "Huh, we're painting the office." Then I turned the corner to discover the most beautiful girl I had ever seen in my life. She was 5'11" and tan, with long, *long* blonde hair, and she was painting the hallway.

All I could do was stare. When she looked over at me, I said, "Hi, how are you?" and quickly walked on by.

When I checked in with the Sales Coordinator, I said, "Hey Melissa, I really approve of Mr. Jenkins' choice of painters. Do you know her name?" Melissa smiled and said, "Her name is Blaire. She just graduated from college, and she's Mr. Jenkins' daughter."

I later learned that she was going to be our first Marketing Director and her desk was pretty close to mine. We struck up a friendship and talked a lot about life and philosophy. It was just an amazing time.

A few months later, I finally gathered up the nerve to ask her out on a date.

I knew Blaire was living back at home with Mr. Jenkins and Reneé, her mother, but it hadn't really soaked in yet that Mr. Jenkins' house is where I'd be picking her up. I've never had a panic attack in my life, but as I was walking up the steps about to ring that doorbell, I felt like my heart was going to jump out of my chest. "Oh crap, I've asked the boss's daughter out on a date, and I really love my job."

We went to a Mexican restaurant and then to a minor league baseball game. It was the perfect summer evening, and I had her home at a respectable hour.

Soon I was a regular at the Jenkins house. I began to get to know Mr. Jenkins and Reneé, and Blaire's sister, Kelly.

Mr. Jenkins told me he was a Petty Officer Second Class in the Navy, an E-5, the equivalent to a sergeant in the Army. He said,

"At sea, you work 12 hours on and 12 hours off, so I was in charge of the night shift for the guys taking care of the electronics on the A-4 aircraft. I didn't know anything about it, hadn't been trained on it, but it taught me to rely on other people. That turned out to be a good experience for me. It gave me confidence in my ability to figure things out, and it gave me trust in other people."

He said, "We were in the Mediterranean on the maiden voyage of the Navy's newest aircraft carrier, the USS John F. Kennedy. I was 21 years old at the time and in charge of guys taking care of multi-million-dollar aircraft. And we could fix them. We'd just grab the manual and figure out how to do it. We were kids working on the flight deck, which is extremely dangerous, but people would look out for you and help you."

His story about grabbing that aircraft manual and "figuring it out" made me feel proud of my giant volume of *Modern Refrigeration and Air Conditioning*. I keep it on a special shelf in my office to this day.

Mr. Jenkins told me that he was from a large family in a small coal-mining town in Southwest Virginia and that his father had been a plumber.

Mr. Jenkins told me that he was selling pots and pans door-to-door on the day he met Reneé and that they moved to Charlotte with only 500 dollars to their names.

I was getting to see a whole other side of Mr. Jenkins.

Blaire and I had been dating for about two years when I saved up enough money to buy a little house. That was when Blaire said to me, "We've been dating for two years. What's your plan?"

I was almost 26 years old.

Mr. Jenkins, Reneé, Blaire, and Kelly were all going to the head-waters of the New River in the mountains of North Carolina for the Fourth of July. The New River runs from North Carolina through Virginia, and by the time it gets to West Virginia, it's a raging river with class four rapids, a really famous river. But here in North Carolina, it's just a nice, wide stream.

I went with them on that trip. Blaire and I took a canoe down the river and found a little island where the river forks to the right and left, but I paddled straight ahead onto the beach. We had a little picnic lunch there, and I asked her to marry me. We came back to the cabin that evening, unveiled our plans, and everyone was happy for us. This was in July, and we said, "Let's get married this fall."

The company had grown to about 80 people by that time and just about everyone showed up for the wedding. Blaire moved in to the little house I had bought, and she put a woman's touch on it.

Over the next few years I became one of the top air conditioning salesmen in America. Every month, the highest volume salesman was either my friend Allen Smith or it was me. Allen and I were intensely competitive, but we were also very close friends and remain so to this day. Our wives are good friends too, and our kids play together. "If I'm not number one, I want Allen to be number one," I would say, and he said the same about me.

When Blaire and I found out we were expecting, we scheduled an ultrasound, and the technician said, "Whoa." Up there on the screen was not one baby, but two. I grabbed a pamphlet on the way out of the office that said, "Are You Expecting Twins?" and I said, "This is how I'm going to tell Mr. Jenkins." So I stuck it in my pocket with that headline sticking out and walked into his office. But he was so focused that he didn't notice it. So I started leaning in and then leaning in some more.

Finally, he looked up and asked, "Why are you leaning in?" I pointed to the brochure. He looked at it, threw his chair back from his desk, threw his arms in the air, and exclaimed, "That's fantastic!" A few months later, Jack and Lily were born, and my little house was filling up quickly.

A few more years went by, and I became a department head.

That was when Mr. Jenkins told me, "People, like diamonds, are made under pressure. But the pressure isn't there to make us crack. It's there to push us to become better."

Not long after that, a doctor said to me, "Jonathan, you have chronic lymphocytic leukemia."

I began to wonder if Mr. Jenkins could see the future.

I had noticed a swollen lymph node on each side of my neck, a little pebble, just before peak air conditioning season was about to begin. I said, "I must be getting a cold or something." A few weeks later, the pebbles were still there. I thought, "I might need to get a checkup."

Dr. Bradford said, "It's probably nothing, but we'll take a little blood." Then he said, "There's one blood marker here that's a little out of whack." So he referred me to a doctor in a big medical plaza in downtown Charlotte. As I was walking into the building, I looked up, and the sign said, "Levine Cancer Institute."

"Uh-oh."

After the doctor looked at me and said, "Jonathan, you have chronic lymphocytic leukemia," I remember sitting in a dark room, stunned, thinking about my early childhood in Camden, a perfectly beautiful, small Southern town, where I had precious memories of the miles and miles of pine forests and my dog, a Llewellin Setter named Dixie, who would run beside me as I would ride my bike down the logging roads through those gorgeous pine trees.

I remembered my suddenly widowed mother, 30 years old with a 7-year-old and a baby, trying to close down my dad's practice. It took her a year and a half to do it, but she moved us back to Charlotte where her parents and my father's parents were. It was the middle of my third-grade year. I remembered fishing with my dad. I remembered fishing with him.

But that was long ago, and memories fade.

When I told Blaire, we had a good cry. Neither of us knew what to expect. But when Mr. Jenkins found out, he spent an entire weekend researching my disease. Blaire and I couldn't do it.

He came over to our house and announced what he had learned. The M.D. Anderson Cancer Center in Houston was the leading research and treatment facility in the world for the type of leukemia that I had. We trusted his advice and his judgment and went exactly where he told us to go. I fought that disease like a tiger for four years. Not only did I get complete remission, but I got what's called "Negative Minimal Residual." It's the best result you can hope for.

Sure, I could get hit by a bus tomorrow, but I don't think about it anymore. If it comes back one day, we've already got Plan B in place.

"Pressure isn't there to make you crack. It's there to push you to become better."

What I learned as I sat in that dark room, stunned, was that it's not really your accomplishments, or your wealth, that make you happy. It's the relationships you have with people who have been with you in the darkness.

Kelly, Reneé, Blaire, and Jonathan on the bank of the New River shortly after Jonathan proposed to Blaire

Jonathan with "Having Twins" brochure

Mr. Jenkins with twins, Lily and Jack

Mr. Jenkins Told Me...

"Don't Lose Your Faith in People."

Worry happens when you begin to contemplate a negative thought.

Hope and belief and confidence happen when you fill your mind with images of a positive outcome and a happy future.

As we emerged from the darkness of my leukemia battle, I said, "Mr. Jenkins, you seem to have a magical ability to lead people upwards to levels they never believed they could go. How do you do that?"

Mr. Jenkins told me, "Never give up on your belief in humanity, Jonathan. Each of us is uniquely and wonderfully made. Accept a person for who they are. Each of us comes into this world full of possibilities, with gifts and talents and unrealized potential. It's your responsibility, and mine, to look for those talents and the goodness that exists in each person and to inspire them to put those talents to use."

"But sometimes people do bad things."

"People do bad things because human nature is conflicted. We have good impulses and bad impulses. The good impulses entice us to do acts of selflessness and love and kindness. The bad impulses entice us to be selfish and destructive. Moment by moment, each of us has to choose which impulse to follow. And everyone around us is faced with those same choices."

"So how do you bring out the good in people?"

"Number one, always assume positive intent."

"What do you mean?"

"Always remember that a person can create a negative result without *intending* to. So give people the benefit of the doubt. Assume that they meant well, until it becomes crystal clear that they didn't."

I felt like what he was saying might be a little too lofty for me to reach, so I asked, "Mr. Jenkins, what have you learned as a leader that you didn't know when you were first starting out?"

"Primarily, to respect people. To be patient with them. And don't try to change them. They are who they are. Respect them and allow them to be themselves, because people *feel good* if they can be themselves. But if they come to work, and they have to pretend to be someone else, it's just a miserable way to live. People who are pretending aren't going to do themselves, or you, any good."

"So have faith in people? Accept them for who they are?"

Mr. Jenkins just smiled and nodded.

After a few long moments, he said, "We look at people, and we think they're just like us, when actually, they are very different. Then when we realize that they're different, we try to change them. But if you accept people for who they are, you get their very best efforts, because you're not criticizing them every day, and you're not trying to make them into somebody else. So let people be who they are."

Mr. Jenkins waited quietly while I pondered. Then, after a couple of minutes, he said, "Do you remember Kitty McCarter, from when you first came to work here?"

Thinking about Kitty, I started laughing. But it was a happy laugh.

Mr. Jenkins said, "Kitty was instrumental to our success. She practically ran the service department by herself for the first seven years I owned the business. Sure, she was quirky and had some rough edges. But we accepted her as she was, and she gave us the best that she had every day."

I finally understood what he was telling me.

"Mr. Jenkins, whatever happened to her?"

"Well, she passed away a couple of years ago. I'm proud to have known her."

That's when it hit me. I said, "I think I'm beginning to understand our staff meetings."

That made Mr. Jenkins smile. "Meetings and communication are the heart of a business, so there needs to be a rhythm to it. I discovered this by accident when I began having weekly meetings right after I bought the company, primarily because I didn't know any of my people. I needed to know them, and I felt they needed to know me. What I found is that there were a lot of good people in our industry that hadn't been treated well."

"Not treated well how?"

"Generally, they were chewed out, told to go out and work harder and work faster and at the end of the day when they came back in, they'd be chewed out again. Everyone had similar stories to tell, no matter where they had worked previously. Chewing people out seemed to be standard operating procedure in the air conditioning business."

"So that's why the focus of every meeting is to keep people informed about what's going on and to give them positive feedback."

Mr. Jenkins smiled when he said, "You're right, Jonathan. You do understand our staff meetings."

"You said a minute ago that meetings had to have a rhythm because meetings and communication are the heartbeat of a company. What is the right rhythm?"

"First, keep everyone informed as to what's happening. They need to know they're important enough to be kept in the loop. Then give them positive feedback. When you get a happy call from a customer or a really positive online review, read those to your team with pride during the meeting, and be sure to publicly recognize the people who made those customers so happy."

"What you're going to find is that this will create a sort of feedback loop. When you praise good performance, your people will give you more good performance to praise. But if you break the rhythm, if you go a few weeks without publicly praising good performance, you'll find you have less good performance to praise. Praise gives people wings, and appreciation gives them the energy to rise up high and see the world from a new perspective."

Kitty McCarter ran the Service Department during the early years

CHAPTER

6

Mr. Jenkins Told Me...

"Celebrate, Celebrate, Celebrate!"

Mr. Jenkins told me, "Traditions are important. Traditions help us remember who we are, which becomes especially important during turbulent times. Traditions gives us a strong sense of identity, which is a powerful glue that can bind us together and make us strong when the storms are blowing. And the most important tradition of all is to celebrate. Celebrate everything that you would like to see happen more often."

"Mr. Jenkins, would you say that celebration is a form of praise?"

"That never occurred to me but now that you say it, I can see that you're right. Celebration is praise taken to its highest level. This is why celebration is our first and highest tradition."

One of our traditions is to celebrate our top performers in each department in a company-wide Champions Gala. This is a distinction that anyone can win, and the constant reinforcement of, "this is the kind of service company we are, and this is the kind of service we deliver," lifts the performance of the entire team to a new level.

When you visit the Morris-Jenkins headquarters building in Charlotte, you'll notice a wall in our most highly trafficked hallway covered in large, expensive photos of our annual champions, year by year. This Champions Gallery gives you a visual sense of the history and heritage of the company.

Mr. Jenkins told me, "You can't mandate a high level of performance. You can only inspire it."

A second tradition is to read the positive comments from customers in every meeting: the Service Technician meetings, the Installation Crew meetings, the Call Center meetings, the Supervisors meetings, the Managers meetings, and the Directors meetings.

Mr. Jenkins told me, "If your employees think you're having too many meetings, then you're not doing it right. The meetings should be fun."

A third tradition is the tradition of learning. The sharing of a new insight or a new skill or a new perspective is part of every meeting, so that people feel enriched and empowered when they leave. You walk into meetings knowing that you're going to feel smarter and stronger and happier when you walk out.

Another way we express our tradition of learning is through our Tech Builder program that takes place in a huge classroom with a high ceiling in the center of our building that is filled with every kind of air conditioner. And every A/C is fully functional. This is where our technicians receive ongoing education through hands-on problem solving.

Each day, our technical trainer will bring a group of technicians into the room and assign each of them an air conditioner to repair. Their job is to correctly diagnose and repair the problem, usually by isolating the faulty part the technical trainer secretly installed before they came into the room. But I remember walking through the room one day to see pairs of technicians working on the units, with one of the them looking at a smart phone and calling out instructions while the other had his head inside the unit. I grinned and asked the technical trainer, "What have you got them doing?"

"I told them that vandals stole all the wiring in the air conditioner and the homeowner didn't have the manual that came with the system."

My eyes got big, and my jaw dropped.

The technical trainer continued, "It took these technicians less than a minute to realize they could pull up factory wiring diagrams on their cell phones and replace every wire in the system."

That's what we call "a tradition of learning." The objective is to have technicians who can always solve the customer's problem quickly and efficiently. And in the A/C business, that's harder than you might suspect.

A fourth tradition is that the company president handwrites and mails a personalized greeting card to every employee on the anniversary date of their employment. It's our way of celebrating that they decided to come and work with us. The employee rarely remembers the date, which makes it all the more important that we do. It's a meaningful way of saying, "You're important to us, and we're really glad you're here."

Can you imagine doing that for 434 employees every year?

I mentioned to Mr. Jenkins that maybe we could cut back on that. I said, "Certainly our people would understand."

But Mr. Jenkins shook his head no. "That's not the one you give up."

"So what would be the tradition to give up?"

"None of them," he smiled. "Work can get kind of mundane. So celebrate, celebrate, celebrate every victory, even the small ones. And do it consistently. It changes the whole atmosphere when you do that. People begin looking for things they can celebrate."

Celebrating a record breaking month with top performers. Chuck is in the back row on the far left

Longtime employees Dave Hearne, Scott Stallings, and Terry Sigmon with awards received at Company Breakfast

Mr. Jenkins raising a toast to celebrate reaching 10,000 Priority Advantage members

Celebrating top performers at our Annual Champions Gala

CHAPTER

7

Mr. Jenkins Told Me...

"Don't Wrestle with Pigs."

As I was thinking of one particular person who made my life difficult during my battle with cancer, I said, "Mr. Jenkins, you tell me to believe in people and let them be who they are, but what do you do when someone is acting like a bastard?"

"Well, that's the hardest thing in the world. Sometimes you work with people, you love them, and then they disappoint you by doing something that is hurtful or dishonest. The temptation then is to build walls around yourself, so you won't ever be hurt again. The hardest thing in the world is not to give up on humanity just because someone has disappointed you. Because if you give up on humanity, if you quit believing in people, you'll end up hurting everyone else because of what that one person did to you."

"But does the time ever come when you finally just give up on a person?"

Mr. Jenkins thought about that for a moment, then said, "No, there's never a time when you give up hoping for the best for them. But sometimes you do have to send them ahead to begin the next chapter of their journey without you. Sometimes you'll have the right person in the wrong job, or you'll have the right person in the right job at the wrong time."

"I'm not sure I understand."

"Jonathan, when a football coach sees that it's 4th and long, what does he do?"

"He punts the football to the other end of the field."

"That's right. He lets the other team have it for a while. Sometimes you have to do that. You have to send a person ahead to the next chapter of their journey. But even then, you never quit believing in their potential. You never quit hoping for the best for them."

The person who had made my life so difficult during my battle with cancer was our technical trainer. He reported to me, and he and I had a close relationship. I considered him a friend.

But while I was out of town for a few days fighting for my life, a competitor offered him more money. He was gone when I came home. His leaving didn't make any sense to me, but in my heart I wished him well and was hoping for the best for him. Then, over the next several weeks, I began to notice that we were losing a technician a week. They would just leave their truck in the parking lot and their keys at the front desk. No notice. No explanation.

None of this made any sense, and no one was talking to me about it.

Finally, one of our employees told me that my friend, the technical trainer, was calling our service technicians and saying, "Mr. Jenkins is getting older, so he's going to be gone, and Jonathan's got cancer, so he's going to die..."

He was scaring our technicians into believing that our company was going down. His message was, "The ship is sinking, so you had better find yourself a new job before the market is flooded with out-of-work air conditioning technicians."

And it just so happened, of course, that his new employer was hiring.

I felt betrayed by my friend, but I didn't want to let that feeling take root in me, so I began to contemplate what I might have done differently. That's when I realized I had treated my cancer like it was a private thing because I was thinking, "This is not something we can celebrate, and it's not a new skill or technique or new perspective to share in our meetings," so I didn't share it because I didn't want to bring everyone down. But now it occurred to me that the principle I had failed to follow was, "Keep everyone informed as to what's happening. They need to know they're important enough to be kept in the loop."

That's where I had gone wrong.

So I spent the next three days attending every staff meeting in the company, which had now grown to about 250 people, and I told each of them that I had leukemia, but that I also had a treatment plan and everything was going well.

I thought about calling my friend to let him know that what he was saying was untrue and what he was doing was wrong. But as I was getting into my truck at the end of the third day, I saw Chuck getting into his truck next to mine. So I told him what was happening and said that I was going to call my friend, the ex-technical trainer, and talk to him.

Chuck just shook his head. "I'm not saying that man is an idiot, but I figure he can get the job done 'til a real one comes along. No, Jonathan, I don't think you should call him. Anyone that would leave this company is proof that a village somewhere is missing its idiot. And trying to have a conversation with an idiot is like playing chess with a pigeon. Sooner or later they're just going to poop on the board and then strut around like they won." Chuck shook his head again. "Don't call him."

That's Chuck. You've got to love him. Especially if one of your core values is to accept people as they are and not try to change them.

The next day I told Mr. Jenkins what I was thinking of doing.

Mr. Jenkins told me, "Don't wrestle with pigs. You're only going to get muddy, and *they like to get muddy*. Your friend is following bad impulses right now. He's in the mud, and there's probably nothing you can do to pull him out of it. Maybe in the future you'll be able to talk to him, but right now is not the time, because it's unlikely that he would be able to hear what he needs to hear."

We walked out of his office. Mr. Jenkins began walking one way, and I was walking the other way when I heard him say, "Jonathan." I turned around to see that he was coming back toward me. "Very few of the difficult people you encounter will be co-workers. More often, they'll be customers."

That was the day I finally understood our "Never argue with the customer" service policy.

Mr. Jenkins said, "Ninety-seven percent of your customers will be wonderful people, but about three percent will believe that every transaction has to have a winner and a loser. And they're going to figure out a way to make sure that you're the loser. They go to sleep at night thinking about it. They wake up in the morning thinking about it. They talk to people at lunch about it. And you're never going to get through to those people that what they're doing is wrong."

"I'm telling you this because most business people spend all their energy fighting with that three percent of their customers, and that's why they fail to grow. So don't wrestle with them. Let them win. Cast it out of your mind and go on with your life."

When all was said and done, that rascal of a technical trainer did us a favor. After he had pulled away all of our employees that he could, the culture of our company began to glow like a light bulb. The best and the brightest and the most deeply committed were what we had left. That's when things began to rocket upward for us, and they've never quit accelerating.

CHAPTER

8

Mr. Jenkins Told Me...

"A Strong Culture Allows Your Business to Move Quickly."

W hen your business has a strong culture, your people know what to expect. And when they know what to expect, they know how to behave in any situation they find themselves in. If you don't have that strong culture, the only way you can get any kind of consistency is to have a set of rules and regulations to cover every situation. But rules and regulations slow people down because they don't know how to react. They have to go back and see what the regulation is, or call a supervisor, before they know what to do."

I'm always amazed at the things Mr. Jenkins tells me.

He said, "A strong culture in a business is like a strong culture in a family. You don't have detailed rules and regulations written down for a family. The family knows, 'This is how we behave. This is what we do.'"

But it was what he said next that surprised me the most. "A business left to its own devices will become complicated. It just shouts for complexity: 'give us rules, give us regulations.' But complexity chokes growth. If we don't continually focus on eliminating complexity, there won't be any growth, because complexity makes it difficult for your customer to do business with you. Complexity makes it difficult for your team to perform at its highest level. I learned from Verne Harnish that when a business doubles its size, the complexity doesn't just double, it increases by a factor of 12. And I've seen this to be true."

I learned from Mr. Jenkins that if you want your company to be able to grow quickly, you must build a strong culture on the consistent celebration of values and beliefs.

But the thing that will sneak up on you and try to hold you down is complexity.

Complexity is like Entitlement, the evil E. It is always there. It surrounds you, and it tries to carve itself into your bones. And if it can do that, it will destroy you.

Mr. Jenkins told me, "The goal is to create a company that can move elegantly and swiftly, like a swan gliding across a lake. But never forget that below the waterline that swan is paddling with everything she's got. Complexity is difficult, but that doesn't mean simplicity is easy. It's hard work to make things elegant and simple and beautiful. But that's what we're here to do. We want the complexity to be behind the curtain and never seen or felt by the customer."

We needed to hire some technicians to replace the ones who had followed our former technical trainer. So I put together a big team of key people to greet new job applicants and move them from station to station, interviewer to interviewer, sort of like speed dating.

Our first-tier interviewers would look for a specific characteristic. If they found it, they would escort that applicant along with their job application to a second-tier interviewer down the hall, where a second interviewer would begin another friendly conversation to determine if the applicant had the additional qualities we value highly.

But if the first-tier interviewer didn't find what they were looking for, they would lift up the application with a smile to show the job applicant that we had it, thank them for filling it out, and then give them a parting gift—a bag full of goodies—and say, "Thanks for coming. It was great to meet you. I hope to see you again."

This simple process moved applicants from station to station quickly, so that no one had to wait very long to be interviewed. There were more first-tier and second-tier interviewers than third- and fourth-tier interviewers, but this was because fewer applicants would make it to the later stations.

The good news is that the only people our former trainer had been able to mislead were the weakest of the people he had been training. Our best and brightest were all still with us, and they knew exactly what kind of people would fit our culture.

The rest of the city had seen our true colors as well.

We made a simple announcement on a Thursday that Morris-Jenkins was ready to hire 10 air conditioning technicians, and any technician who was interested should be at our place at 8 a.m. on Saturday. This was during a time when A/C technicians were in short supply and virtually impossible to find, which explains why our ex-technical trainer was working so hard to lure people away from us.

One hundred and forty-one qualified A/C technicians were waiting in line at 8 a.m.

Problem solved.

A great culture gives you big advantages, one of which is that it allows you to move fast. A bad culture weighs you down with cumbersome rules and regulations.

Mr. Jenkins taught me how to build a great culture.

1. Accept people as they are.
2. When someone makes a mistake, assume positive intent.
3. Publicly praise good performance.
4. Celebrate every good thing that happens. Celebrate, Celebrate, Celebrate!
5. Create meaningful traditions.

And now, you know how to build one, too.

Celebrating the awarding of Supreme Service Champion rings to our Service Champions

Part of the management team celebrating our annual Ugly Sweater Breakfast which quickly grew to include more than just sweaters

Mr. Jenkins Told Me...

"Conflict Happens at Intersections."

W e're told as children that conflict is bad, and we believe it. But conflict is neither good nor bad. It's just a normal part of human interactions. How conflict is managed determines whether it's good or bad.

Conflict is a reality. There is conflict in every relationship. But most people have never been taught how to confront conflict and deal with it. When you've taught your people how to deal with conflict, friction declines, productivity accelerates, people learn to appreciate each other, and your whole organization leaps forward. Because now we get to hear both sides. We have two perspectives and two viewpoints.

And people learn they don't have to be silent. They have an opinion, they have good thoughts, and their opinion and their thoughts matter.

Mr. Jenkins told me, "Crashes occur at intersections. If you look at traffic flow, that's where most of the crashes occur. And it's the same thing in a business. Conflict occurs at intersections, where one person is passing work over to the next person or one department is passing work over to another department."

In the air conditioning business, this can be where a salesperson has sold the job and now they're passing it over to the installation team and the installers say, "You didn't give us all the information. That's why we were unprepared when we arrived," or it can be any one of a thousand other situations where one person becomes frustrated by the actions of another.

The way to handle conflict is to be assertive. So here's what we tell our people:

1. Don't be a victim.
2. But don't be the schoolyard bully, either.

3. Say, "You have needs, and I have needs, too. Let's figure out how we can both get what we need."

When you're assertive, you're saying, "Hey, I'm playing in this game too. You've got to respect me. You've got to listen to me."

When you learn to be assertive and confront conflict, you develop respect for yourself and you build deep relationships with your co-workers.

The key is to make sure that everyone in the company has received exactly the same training. If friction among co-workers rises to the level of management, it's time to reinforce healthy interaction.

And then, when everyone is back on track again, celebrate.

10

Mr. Jenkins Told Me...

"Marketing is the Price You Pay For Your Lack of Operational Excellence."

Operational excellence is built around the idea that people don't fail, systems fail.

An operationally excellent company will have systems in place for recruitment, training, encouragement, and recognition. And it will have systems for scheduling, pricing, communication, delivery and installation, and customer satisfaction.

Mr. Jenkins told me, "If we were perfect in our operations, our customers would do so much marketing for us that we wouldn't be able to handle all the business. Now that's not to degrade marketing. I love marketing, as you know. But our most effective marketing isn't about the products and services we sell. Our most effective marketing shares our core values and beliefs so that our customers can bond with us. They say, 'Hey, I believe what you believe.' And then they remember our company when they need us."

"But what if their values don't align with our values?"

"Then that customer is probably not going to call us."

"But why would we create ads that keep some people from calling us?"

"A message that is strong enough to move people will move a few of them in the wrong direction. So most businesses play it super-safe, and that's why their ads don't work very well."

"Running ineffective ads is 'playing it safe'?"

"Most ads aren't written to persuade," said Mr. Jenkins, "they're written not to offend. But we don't write super-safe ads because we choose not to worry about the 3% who will misinterpret our message and give us grief about it."

"Is this another example of not wrestling with pigs?"

"Jonathan, do you remember the TV ad where we suggested that women should consider a career as an air conditioning technician?"

"It's one of the best ads we ever ran."

"It also made some people angry." Mr. Jenkins then pulled open a file drawer, slid that TV script from its folder, and laid it down in front of me.

Tech ONE - Sadie: Mr. Jenkins told me...

Tech TWO - Deleanna: Mr. Jenkins told me...

Tech THREE - Lynda: Mr. Jenkins told me...

Tech ONE - Sadie: The world needs more female

Tech FOUR - Heather: air conditioning technicians.

Tech FIVE - Chris: It's a really good job. [Insert a quick shot of Sadie and Chris smiling as they give each other a fist bump.]

Tech TWO - Deleanna: Morris-Jenkins has their own training school.

Tech SIX - Jeremy: And they'll work with you to help get you [pointing to the Morris-Jenkins "Supreme Service Champion" patch on his shoulder] **certified.**

Tech THREE - Lynda: You'll solve problems for people every day.

Tech TWO - Deleanna: And that feels GOOD.

Tech FOUR - Heather: You can move your family to a better neighborhood.

Tech SIX - Jeremy: That feels good, too.

Mr. Jenkins: The world DEFINITELY needs more
female technicians.

CLOSING SHOT: [Morris-Jenkins headquarters
illuminated at night]

I read that script carefully. "But Mr. Jenkins, what could a person possibly complain about?"

"That's exactly the question most business owners ask themselves before releasing an ad to the public. And then, when the business owner gets a few complaints, he thinks, 'Oh, we've made a horrible mistake!' and they replace that ad with something that's easier to ignore."

"Anyone who would complain about that ad would have to have a pretty low IQ."

"Actually, IQ isn't the problem. It's usually their EQ that's below average."

I must have had a puzzled look on my face.

"EQ, or emotional intelligence, is the ability to correctly monitor your own emotions and the emotions of others and to use that information to guide your thinking and behavior. A person who routinely misinterprets the words and actions of other people usually has a low EQ. And that's a much bigger problem than having a low IQ."

"How so?"

"Your EQ determines how you deal with people, and how you deal with people determines your success. If you look at studies that have been done, the people with the highest IQ are generally not as successful as those with a high EQ. They're the ones who know how to work with people. They're the people who get things done."

That was the moment I finally understood the interview process we use in hiring new employees. Technical skills will get the job done, but EQ makes the customer feel good about having chosen you.

Technical skills give you the ability to deal with objects.

Emotional skills give you the ability to deal with people.

We always look for a healthy EQ.

Billboard supporting our TV ads recruiting female Technicians

Mr. Jenkins Told Me...

"Leadership Isn't Management."

What most people do, generally, is elevate the role of leadership and denigrate the role of manager. Most people feel the role of a leader is higher than that of a manager. But really they're just two different roles."

I asked Mr. Jenkins to explain the difference.

"The role of a manager is to turn talent into performance. It's to look at each person individually and then put them in a position where they can work to their strengths. If you put a person in an area where they're strong, you get tremendous, tremendous performance. But if you try to work on their weaknesses, you get a tiny little bit of improvement. So the manager's job is to look inwardly and recognize the talents of each individual."

I nodded that I understood.

"A leader's job, on the other hand, is to look outwardly with the employee. The leader's role is to show each person a better future. A leader's message is always, 'Tomorrow is going to be better than today.' Everyone has uncertainty about the future. This is why a good leader will say, 'Here is where we're going, and this is how we're going to get there.' In truth, the leader may not know exactly how they are going to get there, but if he can paint that picture and give people hope, his team will follow him anywhere."

I asked, "So if management and leadership are two separate things, why do most people think they're the same?"

Mr. Jenkins said, "Most people believe that managers are made, but leaders are born. How many times have you heard it said that this person or that person is 'a born leader'?"

"I've heard that my whole life."

"Leadership is learned with experience, and it is learned with study. It's not something that you're born with. When people say someone is 'a born leader,' they're usually just impressed with that person's boldness and confidence. But it takes a lot more than boldness and confidence to connect with a person's innermost goals and dreams. It requires a high EQ. People need to know that you care for them and that you have their best interests in mind."

"Does a manager have to have a high EQ as well?"

"Absolutely. A manager provides correction and gives feedback. A good manager will give praise immediately when they see good performance, and if there's something that needs to be corrected, they'll also do that immediately. But the praise will be public, and the correction will be private. And to do that consistently takes a high EQ."

"It's important to be consistent?"

Mr. Jenkins nodded, "If you are consistent, you will earn people's trust, and you can't be an effective manager if your team doesn't trust you."

I was thinking about what Mr. Jenkins had said about praise and correction, so I asked, "Mr. Jenkins, why don't we do annual performance reviews?"

He smiled, "I don't do annual performance reviews because there are easier ways to make people angry."

I laughed.

Mr. Jenkins continued. "A good manager would never wait a year to tell a team member how they're doing. You wouldn't wait a year to tell Blaire how she's doing, would you? Annual reviews wouldn't work well in a marriage, so why do people think they'll work well at the office?"

Mr. Jenkins Told Me...

"Don't Try to Win a Negotiation. A 'Win' is a Fair Deal for All Parties."

I always enjoyed my talks with Mr. Jenkins, but I couldn't help but wonder what he was thinking when he began teaching me how to do things that weren't really in my job description.

In fact, they weren't in the description for any job I ever imagined I'd be doing.

One day, Mr. Jenkins said, "Before I start a negotiation, I always write down and answer these questions:

- What do I really want for myself or for my business?
- What do I want for others?
- What do I want for this relationship?"

He saw that I was writing this down, so he paused until I looked back up at him.

He said, "At its heart, negotiating is about human interactions, not money. Going into a negotiation, a good question to ask is 'How do I reach an agreement with someone whose interests aren't perfectly aligned with mine?' Thinking of it this way provides a different perspective to start with and increases the likelihood that your negotiation will be successful."

I wrote it down, then looked up and nodded that I understood.

Mr. Jenkins continued, "Another advantage of approaching negotiations this way is that it allows you to maintain your focus. When you're involved in a negotiation with a win-lose mentality, you can't help but be wrapped up in emotional turmoil. And this is the enemy of focus. In fact, it destroys focus."

Another look up, another nod.

"Instead of focusing on providing a better customer experience or creating a great culture for your employees, you're locked in a win-lose struggle that typically only escalates. Save your emotional energy for building up your employees and finding new ways to serve your customers."

"This is really good stuff, Mr. Jenkins."

He smiled a little, then said, "Here's something else that most people don't think about. It's the good karma that comes from treating people right. I've bought a number of houses and a number of business properties. I have never gotten a steal. But I have always come out very well on the other side when I've sold the properties. If you go into a transaction with the idea that you're gonna be fair to everyone concerned, I've found it easier to do the deal. Plus, you gain a reputation for fairness, and people will bring other deals to you that you would otherwise never even know about."

Mr. Jenkins told me that of all the things he had ever taught me, the most important one to remember was this: "Always remember that you're dealing with people, and when dealing with people the objective is *almost* always to preserve the relationship. So make it fair."

I said, "*Almost* always?"

I saw the corners of his mouth droop as a little sadness came into his eyes. "Sometimes it's just not an option."

I didn't ask him for details.

Mr. Jenkins Told Me...

"Growth Never Happens in a Vacuum."

M r. Jenkins looked steadily into my eyes and said, "We're a growth company. We set new records almost every month. That's what a growth company does."

He showed me a series of growth charts going back to the very beginning, and then he said, "It's easy to look at charts like those and think, 'It was easier back then; growth was so much simpler. Those were the good old days.' But no, no, no. It was never easy. We were dealing with issues back then that were very similar to what we deal with now. For instance:

- Staffing for a business that jumps up and down with the weather; having the right number of techs to handle 200 service calls on March 15th and then 1400 on July 4th
- Finding people that fit our culture
- Improving systems to make it easier for our employees and customers
- Teaching our employees how to manage conflict in order to make it productive and successful"

He said, "No... it's never been easy. When one problem is solved, another takes its place. And in a growth business, the problem that takes its place is almost always a bigger one. So while it's tempting to look back and say, 'Those were the good old days.' Don't do it."

He looked up from the charts just as I was swallowing a big lump in my throat. And I think my eyes might have been a little bigger than usual. He was talking to me about big responsibilities and big decisions that would affect hundreds of employees and tens of thousands of customers.

I think he knew what I was feeling, so he beamed his biggest smile and said, "Enjoy the moment. It isn't in celebrating the achievement that you develop relationships. It's in the struggle.

You've heard that life isn't found in the destination, but in the journey, right?"

I nodded yes.

I swear I saw his eyes twinkle when he said, "It's true. Enjoy the journey."

"But it's a lot of pressure," I said.

He nodded and said, "Pressure is a good thing."

"I'm not sure what you mean."

"Growth is the result of stress. It never happens in a vacuum. So, what is the opposite of a vacuum?"

I thought for a moment, then snapped my fingers, "A pressure cooker!"

"Business growth happens in a pressure cooker," said Mr. Jenkins, "but the pressure isn't coming from management. The pressure is coming from the marketplace."

"You mean it comes from our competitors?"

"Not usually, but sometimes," said Mr. Jenkins. "More often it's coming from the weather, or from the expectations of customers, or from new regulations, or shortages of materials, or a shortage of qualified people."

I relaxed a little as everything he said started soaking in. "Gosh, Mr. Jenkins, that's nothing new. That's stuff we do every day."

He stood up and smiled a big smile as he shook my hand. "Welcome to the big leagues."

(1990) Reneé and Mr. Jenkins in front of their new business after buying Morris Heating & Cooling

(1995) After outgrowing the original facilities we moved to Center Park Drive and with continued growth eventually occupied two buildings there

(2017) We outgrew those facilities too. Here, some of our employees are saying goodbye to Center Park Drive

(2017) New headquarters building on South Ridge Drive in Charlotte

Mr. Jenkins Told Me...

"Don't Try to Correct Their Weaknesses, Let Each Player Play to Their Strengths."

After he welcomed me to the big leagues, Mr. Jenkins told me, "Focus on each person's strength. I came to understand that after trying, unsuccessfully, to remake people for years. I think you gain wisdom as you get older and have worked with a lot of people. You can't take a person's weakness and turn that into a strength. You can't do that. I can't do that. No one can do that. But we try to. And really, that's a cruel thing to do to a person. What I've found is, if you look at a person carefully, you'll find their strength. And if you put them in a place where they can use that strength every day, they're happy, and they'll come to work energized."

"You get remarkable performance that way."

Then Mr. Jenkins said, "Invariably, when you go to work for someone, they'll want to identify your weaknesses and try to fix them. When you're in that kind of environment and have your annual review, they'll say, 'Now here's where you're weak and you need to work on this. And this time next year, come back and show us that you've worked on this.'"

Mr. Jenkins looked a little disturbed, and then he said, "Think about it. You have a weakness for a reason, and the reason is that you're weak in that area. If you have to spend all your time working on something you're weak on, you're going to be working on something you don't enjoy. And you're never gonna be very good at it. It just doesn't happen. But if I can identify your strength, and I help you work on that strength, you'll get 10 times better at something you really enjoy doing. You'll be a marvel."

I said, "Give me an example."

Mr. Jenkins said, "You were a baseball player, right?"

I smiled and nodded my head. I was proud of my record in baseball.

Mr. Jenkins said, "A baseball player who's both a good hitter and a good fielder is ideal. But a good hitter, even without the best fielding skills, is still going to find his way into the lineup. He's just usually going to be put in left or right field because he has less ground to cover there."

He went on, "Let's take the example of a player like that who hits 30 home runs and isn't a very good fielder. If his manager instructs him to spend all winter working on his fielding, he'll come back next year and hit fewer home runs and still won't be worth a hoot as a fielder. But if his manager says, 'You're the greatest hitter I've ever seen. Man, look at what you did last year! Let's work on that a little bit more!' He'll come back and hit 50 home runs and be the MVP of the league. Never mind that he isn't a very good fielder."

Mr. Jenkins was talking to me in my own language. I knew exactly what he meant. That's when I realized, "He chose baseball because he's talking to me. He would have chosen something else if he was talking to someone who never played baseball."

Mr. Jenkins talks to every person differently. The Golden Rule is, "Do unto others as you would have them do unto you." But Mr. Jenkins takes that a half-step further because he knows that everyone isn't exactly like him. He does unto others *the way they prefer to be done unto.* That's why he was talking to me about baseball. I made a note to always remember that.

He broke me out of my contemplation when he began speaking again. "That doesn't mean that you can always just ignore weaknesses. You have to understand the circumstances. If you have a weakness that's critical to your job, you're probably in the wrong position. But if it's critical to your job, and you still need to be in that job, then you have to find somebody who can cover that weakness for you. If you do that, then you'll be fine."

Someday I hope to be as wise as Mr. Jenkins.

Jonathan passes down his love of baseball by coaching Jack's team

Mr. Jenkins Told Me...

"An Organization Grows Only as Large as the Key People Representing It."

The first time I heard him say it was in a meeting of department heads: "An organization grows only as large as the key people representing it." And then he paused for a moment and looked at us, one at a time. After he had made eye contact with each of us, he finished his thought, "If each of us hires people bigger than we are, we will become a company of giants."

And then he continued, "One of the hardest things to deal with is when a person's job has outgrown their ability. The position has become bigger than they can handle. I've seen this happen many times and for the most part I've not handled it well."

Casey Welch, one of the other department heads, asked, "Not handled it well, how?"

"We work closely with people, and we grow to love them. We get attached to them, no matter what anyone says. They stood with you in the tough times and they did a good job, so as time went on, you began to overlook some things and not hold them accountable. So you wind up with unacceptable performance coming from someone who is really trying. And it's someone you deeply care about."

I spoke up and said, "Someone told me once that if you manage with your head only, and not your heart, you'll wind up running a sweatshop. But if you manage with your heart only, and not your head, you'll wind up running a country club for employees."

Mr. Jenkins nodded his head and continued, "The best answer I've encountered came from a seminar I attended with Thomas Stemberg, the founder of Staples. After he sold Staples, Tom became a venture capitalist, investing in private businesses with rapid growth potential. He said, 'I've learned to be honest with the owners of the companies we're acquiring. I tell them, "We're going to buy your company and put this or that much capital into it, and we want you to run it for us. But you may not be the person to run this company when it reaches a billion dollars in revenues. There's no way for either of us to know that right now. It depends on how you develop. But here's what I will promise you: if you're not the right person to run this company in the future, I'll tell you to your face and I'll treat you humanely. I'll sit down with you and we'll decide where you go from there.'"

Mr. Jenkins went on to say, "I've told some of our people that same thing upfront and it kind of scares them, but I think it's the most honest and loving thing you can tell someone. Because if you have a person in a job that has outgrown them, everyone they work with knows it. And they'll be quietly miserable because they know they're not doing the job anymore."

Mr. Jenkins said, "A moment ago I told you that I haven't always handled that situation well in the past."

I said, "Yes, sir."

"I handled it badly every time I left a person in a position that was no longer right for them or for the company. I should have had the courage to do what was right for both of us."

"So what, exactly, would be the right thing?" I asked.

Mr. Jenkins said, "The humane thing is to let the person know your thoughts and give them an opportunity to improve in a short period of time. And if they don't, give them a severance package and help them find another position." And then he looked at us as seriously as I've ever seen him look. "That is the truly humane thing to do."

"I'm sorry, Mr. Jenkins," I said, "but that just makes my heart hurt. Is there no possible way we can help that person grow into the job that's too big for them?"

I've sometimes wondered if I was worried about those other people, or about myself.

Then Mr. Jenkins answered, and it made sense. "I wish we could, but it's up to that person to grow as the job grows. Our responsibility is to provide support, feedback, training, access to outside resources, and, above all, a nurturing environment. But when all is said and done, it's up to the individual. We can't make them grow. We can only provide an environment conducive to growth."

I nodded my agreement, and Mr. Jenkins continued.

"Something else we haven't talked about is leadership. Today you hear a lot about flat organizations and work teams. Based on all the attention paid to these concepts, you'd think that leadership is no longer important. Well, it is still important. And in this age of rapid change, I would say it's vitally important."

Another nod.

"To understand how deeply the need for leadership is ingrained in us, it's important to first understand that human nature doesn't change. The same passions, emotions, and desires that drove us thousands of years ago drive us today. Consider these ancient examples: Cain killed Abel in anger, Joseph was sold into slavery because of his brother's jealousy, and King David's desire for another man's wife led him to behave badly. Anger, jealousy, and desire remain a part of our nature today. Nothing's changed."

I wasn't sure what to say, so I just kept quiet.

And then he continued, "Just as human nature doesn't change, neither does an organization's need for a good leader and a strong culture. You can trace this back to the beginnings of recorded civilization. The very first organization was the family with the father at its head. Next came the tribe where all the members were related by blood and everyone was a cousin. Those tribes needed a leader and were usually ruled by a tribal elder."

This was beginning to make a lot of sense, so I nodded my head more quickly.

"As tribes began to live near each other, a different structure evolved. And that structure was a Monarchy, a single ruler, usually called a King or Queen."

Now we were on solid footing. I remembered all this from junior high.

"Civilization evolved, but the need for a leader remained. Humans need safety and to be part of a community that makes them feel special. They need authority to shield them from chaos, and they need to feel confident about the future. A leader is responsible for providing those needs. Nothing has really changed."

I said, "Okay. Safety, community, authority, confidence. But how does a leader accomplish all that?"

Mr. Jenkins looked at me and said, "Culture."

That surprised me. "Culture?"

"Yes. Culture, a belief system defined by its norms and values."

"Norms and values?"

"Norms are rules that define appropriate and inappropriate behavior. Values are principles and judgements about what is important in life."

I said, "Can you simplify that for me?"

"In the simplest possible language, culture is 'how we do things around here.' You have a strong culture when things don't have to be thought out. Everyone knows what to do because, 'that's how we do it.'"

"A strong culture gives you predictability—confidence. You can act in an almost unconscious way. A weak culture exacts a great cost in bringing to the conscious mind those decisions that would have been put on autopilot in a strong culture. The cost of a weak culture is indecision and confusion. A weak culture requires a lot of energy and slows you down."

I was all ears as he continued, "Culture translates the beliefs of the group into a common language. In a company, culture is the personality of the brand, the 'human operating system.'"

"The stronger the culture, the fewer rules you need. You can trust everyone to do the right thing. Your people can be independent and autonomous."

"You see, this is the reason that families don't require written rules and regulations. There's such a strong trust and culture that it supersedes any need for detailed instructions."

"On the other hand, a company with a weak culture needs heavy, precise rules and processes. And its reliance on rules and regulations slows it down. It's kind of like driving in the mountains. When your vision is clear, you can go fast. But when its foggy, you have to slow down."

It hit me like a bolt of lightning. "That's why we look for the right people to hire, not just the right resume!"

Mr. Jenkins smiled, "A strong culture will attract people who are like you, people who identify with your values. And it will repel people who are not like you. John Knight, our IT Director, often says, 'If our culture rejects you, it's not us, it's you.'"

Celebrations don't always have to be about achievements. Sometimes they can just be fun. Here we're celebrating Mullet Monday

Morris-Jenkins sponsored radiothon raised over $150,000 for Levine Children's Hospital

The company breakfast is a fun part of the Morris-Jenkins culture

16

Suddenly, I Knew.

Have you ever suddenly known something without knowing how you knew it?

I woke up one morning and knew that Mr. Jenkins was going to make me president of the company. I don't know how I knew it, I just did.

I knew that someday soon he was going to ask me to make big decisions, and I didn't feel ready. So I got serious about acquiring all the remaining gold nuggets of wisdom that I knew he hadn't yet shared.

I'm not saying that Mr. Jenkins had been holding back on me. He wouldn't do that. But it occurred to me that the golden nuggets usually came when I asked for his advice. So I started asking him questions I had never asked before, just to see what they might unleash.

I say 'unleash' because I believe a person's curiosity is more important than their power. Power is about what you can control. Curiosity is about what you can unleash.

I wanted to unleash all the wonderful stories that Mr. Jenkins had not yet told me.

It was the smartest thing I ever did.

CHAPTER 17

Mr. Jenkins Told Me...

"There's No Such Thing as a Bad Opportunity."

M r. Jenkins, how did you know that an air conditioning company was the right business for you to buy?"

Mr. Jenkins paused for a moment, then said, "I don't think of business opportunities as being either good or bad. I just think there are opportunities you choose to act on, and those you don't."

"Well, then how do you know when it's the right time to act?"

"It's always a mistake to wait for the perfect opportunity, just like it's always a mistake to wait for the perfect plan, or to wait for the perfect outcome. Just get started, and then make continual improvements as you go along. Anything worth doing is worth doing imperfectly. If it's truly worth doing, it's worth doing badly until you've gotten better at it."

"You're saying not to let the perfect become the enemy of the good?"

"Exactly. Just get started. And remember that the biggest opportunities often come to you disguised as problems."

It took me a minute to wrap my head around that. Finally, I said, "Can you give me an example of a big opportunity that came to you disguised as a problem?"

Mr. Jenkins said, "I'm not a believer in perfectionism. I'm a believer in doing things, making mistakes, and improving. That's the way you get things done." Then he asked, "How many Priority Advantage members do we have right now?"

I said, "About 24 thousand."

"And how much do they pay us?"

"Nineteen ninety-nine a month."

"And how much did that come to last year?"

"About 5 million, 750 thousand dollars."

"And what do Priority Advantage members get for their $19.99?"

I said, "Twice-a-year routine maintenance, which includes an air conditioner system renovation during the first part of the year and a furnace safety check during the latter part. And they also get discounts when they need repairs, and they're moved to the head of the line when they have a problem. They always get the next available technician."

"Is Priority Advantage a good deal for our customers?"

"It's a fabulous deal for our customers!" I said.

"Why?"

"Because a maintained system lasts longer, breaks down less often, and uses less energy."

"Do you know when that program became successful?"

I shook my head no.

Mr. Jenkins said, "Back when you were still a salesman, we had stalled out at about 4,000 members. Every time we'd add a member, we'd lose a member. It was like a revolving door. The monthly maintenance program was sold by our customer service representatives who worked in the call center, so I called a meeting with the general manager, the service manager, and the supervisor of the call center to see if we could figure out what was holding us back."

I had never heard this story.

Mr. Jenkins continued, "We were probably 45 minutes into the meeting when Debbie, the call center supervisor, said, 'I'll tell you why we don't sell them.' And I said, 'Why?' And Debbie said, 'Because we don't do what we say. We don't keep our word.'"

Mr. Jenkins saw that my eyes were big and my jaw had dropped.

He nodded his head and said, "That was like a dagger in the heart. But I knew she was right. We didn't always give our members the next available technician."

My eyes got even bigger.

Mr. Jenkins continued, "When we got busy and the calls came rolling in, we always took the customers that had the oldest equipment, whether they were a monthly maintenance member or not. And we'd reschedule the maintenance that we owed our maintenance customers because we had all these other emergencies. I told myself that it was okay to do what we were doing because that's the way the air conditioning industry operates. That's the way everybody does it. We were just normal."

"But we had maintenance customers that had been rescheduled four, five times during the summer, and we were wondering why they wouldn't renew. So when Debbie said that, it struck me hard. And I decided that we were going to start doing exactly what we promised, no excuses. If every other company wanted to send their trucks to those higher profit emergency calls, then so be it. But we were going to deliver what we promised."

"But Mr. Jenkins," I said, "Now we're honoring our maintenance commitments AND sending technicians immediately when those crisis calls come in. What changed?"

"I saw the problem as an opportunity."

"And what was that opportunity, exactly?"

"It was an opportunity to hire more technicians and buy more trucks. After I decided that we were going to keep our word, no matter what, I realized that we didn't have a shortage of customers. We had a shortage of technicians."

Training in our lab

Graduation from Tech Builder class is a big deal. Graduates are proud of their diplomas

Celebrating Graduation! Always an exciting day

Families are invited to Graduation and join in the celebrations

CHAPTER EIGHTEEN

More Questions for Mr. Jenkins

I t occurred to me one day that the simplest questions often triggered the best stories, so I said, "Mr. Jenkins, you were raised in Virginia and Reneé was raised in Florida, so what attracted the two of you to Charlotte?"

"I met Reneé when I was based at the Naval Air Station in Jacksonville, Florida. I wanted some additional income, so in the evenings I went door to door selling pots and pans. One of the doors I knocked on was Reneé's. We hit it off immediately and were married a year later."

"Reneé had gone to school in the Shenandoah Valley of Virginia, and she loved the change of seasons. I had grown up in the mountains of Virginia where it snowed and I hated snow, so I loved Florida. But both of us had traveled through the Carolinas and thought that it was pretty. There was no internet at that time, so I went to the library and found some information about the Carolinas. Then we visited Charlotte and Asheville, but Asheville felt a bit too small for us."

"What year would that have been?"

"I got out of the Navy in September of '71 and in those days, when your enlistment expired, the Navy would move you anywhere in the country you wanted to go. We only had two rooms of furniture, but with the Navy paying for it, at least we could take it with us. We had never had anyone move us before, so we assumed that if we could drive to Charlotte in a day, they could too, or they would at least be there the next day. But they didn't show up until eight days later, so we slept on the floor with just a blanket." He smiled. "We were naïve kids."

"Did you have jobs lined up?"

"No, and our life savings was a total of $500. But Reneé was a dental assistant so she found a job right away, and I found a job in a warehouse. It was the distribution center for Chrysler Airtemp. Chrysler was making air conditioning equipment back in those days, and they had a little one-man warehouse and I was that man. Fresh out of military service, I enjoyed being in charge of myself. That's when I started going to school at night to complete my college degree, but I quickly realized, 'This is going to take forever.' I quit that job and started going to school full-time, but I couldn't quit without any income, so I started a janitorial company."

My eyes got big again. Mr. Jenkins is a wealthy, respected man in our community. "You were a janitor?"

"The people at Chrysler Airtemp really liked me so they became my first janitorial customer. Then I picked up three other buildings right around them and later picked up a few others. I worked at night and on weekends cleaning offices, and I was making a lot more money than my friends who were working at McDonalds. Plus, I had my freedom."

Mr. Jenkins never said it, but I knew the reason the people at Chrysler Airtemp liked him was because he took his passion with him wherever he went. As I listened to him speak, it dawned on me that a person can become successful at anything they choose to do. Success isn't about choosing the right career path. It's about choosing to be the right kind of person.

"What was your major in college?" I asked.

"I had to come out of college with a job, so my major needed to be something that would definitely get me one when I graduated. So I started looking in the help wanted ads to see what it was companies were looking for. I saw a lot of ads for accountants, so I said, 'That's me. I'm going to become an accountant with a CPA.'"

When Mr. Jenkins told me his original plan was to be a CPA, he was teaching me, "If Plan A doesn't work, that's okay, as long as you're ready to launch Plans B, C, and D."

I said, "I'll bet you graduated at the top of your class."

"I had the highest scholastic average in the accounting department, all A's with the exception of one B in my last semester. Applied Management Science. It wasn't really difficult, but I spent my time studying for my CPA exam during that final semester, because to me the CPA exam was the most important."

"Did you pass it on your first attempt?"

Mr. Jenkins nodded. "I had a lot of job offers, which is exactly what I wanted. But what I didn't know is that, while every large accounting firm wanted to hire me, none of them offered rapid advancement, no matter how well you performed. It was the standard two years to make Senior Accountant, five years to make manager, and ten to fifteen years to make partner."

"But I wasn't a kid anymore. I had spent four years in the Navy, the last two supervising a team responsible for the repair of sophisticated, multi-million-dollar aircraft. I had started and run my own janitorial business. Reneé and I had worked hard to pay for my college education. Five years to make manager and ten to make partner seemed like a slow process, so when I saw an opportunity to launch my own tax practice, I decided to take it."

"I started with just a few clients and worked to build the practice. And then Blaire was born, so Reneé quit her job to become a stay-at-home mom. I was now the sole provider for our family and what I earned from the tax practice wasn't enough, so in addition to the tax practice I took a part-time position at The University of North Carolina-Charlotte, teaching accounting. My routine was both exhilarating and exhausting."

"Later, after I had built the practice, a friend from the large accounting firm joined me, and we formed a partnership specializing in real estate accounting and tax. We grew to love real estate because of the opportunities it presented. So we sold the accounting practice and used what we got from the sale as seed money to develop a 260-unit apartment community."

"Then boom. The rug got pulled out from under us. It turned out that we weren't the only ones to see the potential for apartments in a growing area like Charlotte. National builders saw the opportunity too and built so many units that the market was flooded. Our vacancies went through the roof."

"Worse yet, we completed a market research study and concluded that Charlotte wouldn't absorb all those vacancies for another five or six years. We couldn't go that long without building another project. We needed the income."

"So, just like that, we were out of business and at the edge of being broke. There I was; 39 years old, married, with two little girls and a little bit of savings, but not much. I had to do something."

"Luckily, I had a friend in the securities business, and he offered me a job calling on businesses that had retirement plans. But I'm not really a salesperson at heart. I can make myself do it, but I'm not really a salesman. But I did that for a couple of years and learned a lot from it. Most importantly, though, I got to meet a lot of successful business people who cared enough about their employees to create a retirement plan for them. That's when I began looking for a business to buy."

I was glad I had asked the question because these stories were filling in a lot of blanks for me. I nodded eagerly to keep Mr. Jenkins talking.

"I wanted a business that would be able to survive a recession. Originally, I was looking for a plumbing business because people will pay for plumbing even when money is tight. If the toilet stops up, they're going to pay to have that drain unclogged."

I nodded and said, "That sounds like solid thinking."

"Then I got a call from a business broker who said, 'I've got a business I think you ought to look at.' It was a heating and air conditioning business, but I knew that it gets hot and humid in Charlotte and that people will pay for air conditioning just like they pay for plumbing. So I bought Morris Heating and Cooling Company."

"What year was that?" I asked.

"1990."

I was beginning to understand what Mr. Jenkins had said about business opportunities being neither good nor bad. You choose to act on an opportunity, or you choose not to. Success doesn't come when you follow your passion. Success comes when you bring your passion to what you've chosen to do.

Don't follow your passion. Follow your opportunity.

I slowly shook my head back and forth in amazement. "So you got into air conditioning from selling employee retirement plans to business owners..."

Mr. Jenkins nodded and said, "For the first 15 years, I worked six days a week. Sometimes seven. And Reneé would come in and do whatever needed to be done. If we needed help on the telephones, she would do that. If we needed help with warranties, she would do warranties. Blaire was 13, and Kelly was 10. They would come in on the weekends and clean the office. But never together. I would bring each of them in on an every-other-week basis. I paid them $7 a week. They got $5 in cash, and I'd put $2 into savings. They cleaned those offices right up until they went to college."

I said, "I guess if their father had worked cleaning offices on evenings and weekends, they could too, huh?"

Mr. Jenkins nodded, "And during the hot summer months, they would catch us up on filing because we were so busy that we didn't have time to file anything. Back then, we kept paper files by street address. Our technicians would come back from jobs with paper tickets and just pile them up for Blaire and Kelly to organize. They both hated it. They still say it's the worst job they ever had."

"But one summer Kelly had a job she really loved. She worked in our warehouse as a parts runner. When a technician needed a part, she'd hop in a truck and drive it out to them. She loved driving those old trucks. Then, after college, Kelly became our first Human Resources Director. And Blaire, as you know, became our first Marketing Director and continued in that job right up until she had the twins."

Then Mr. Jenkins smiled as he said, "But you already knew that."

Mr. Jenkins on flight deck of USS John F Kennedy in front of an A-4 Skyhawk

Reneé and Mr. Jenkins on their wedding day

Blaire and Kelly, Mr. Jenkins' daughters, cleaned the offices and shop every weekend during the early years

Mr. Jenkins, Reneé, Jack, Lily, Blaire, Kelly, and Jonathan after a meeting honoring Mr. Jenkins with the Distinguished Rotarian Award

Mr. Jenkins Told Me...

"Your Thoughts and Your Companions Shape the Kind of Person You're Becoming."

P eople take only those actions they've already seen in their minds. First, we imagine doing something. Then we do it. We don't take actions we haven't thought of.

If you think about something repeatedly, you bring yourself right up to the brink of doing it. That final step—action—is a tiny one when you've already done it repeatedly in your mind.

It's important that we imagine ourselves doing the right things, not the wrong ones.

This is what Mr. Jenkins told me.

Likewise, your choice of companions is important because they influence your behavior by causing you to imagine things you might not otherwise have imagined.

Do your companions cause you to imagine productive things, or unproductive ones?

One day I said to Mr. Jenkins, "You've always said anything worth doing is worth doing imperfectly until you've learned to do it better. So how do you reconcile that with being a perfectionist?"

Both of his eyebrows were raised as Mr. Jenkins smiled. "You think I'm a perfectionist?"

I made a casual gesture as I looked up and down the hallway. "We all do."

He shook his head. "I think you're confusing perfectionism with preparation. I'm not a perfectionist, but I never under-prepare. Or at least I don't feel good when I do, so I'll admit to being organized. But a perfectionist, at heart, is someone who doesn't want to be hurt. They think, 'I'm going to do this perfectly so that nobody can say anything bad about me. If I do it perfectly, they'll never hurt me on this.' A perfectionist doesn't trust other people. A perfectionist feels good only if he or she has complete control.

I was a perfectionist when I was younger, but then I realized that it's better to work as a team and accept everyone as they are."

I said, "It all comes down to working together as a team to make it easy for customers to do business with us."

Mr. Jenkins nodded, "Do you remember why we launched our plumbing division?"

I remembered it well. When our technicians were inspecting the A/C ductwork in the crawlspace beneath a home, they would often see evidence of a water leak from a faucet or a drain. So they always took a photo of it and showed it to the homeowner as a courtesy. But then the homeowner would almost always ask, "Do you know a good plumber you can recommend?"

I replied to Mr. Jenkins, "We started Morris-Jenkins Plumbing because we were worried about recommending someone who might disappoint our customer."

Mr. Jenkins nodded his agreement as he said, "We launched our plumbing division as an expression of our values, our commitment to the customer. But telling them about a problem that we weren't prepared to solve added an element of customer frustration to our visit, and we just couldn't let that stand."

"I remember the day we made that decision," I said. "And I've always been proud of it."

"Me too. Another thing I've always been proud of is that back in 2009, during the greatest recession of our lifetime, we laid no one off. We cut back on things, but we didn't cut back on people. That was another time we communicated our values through our actions, not just our words."

I wanted to give Mr. Jenkins a high-five right then, but he's not really a high-five kind of guy. So I said, "And that move has really paid off for us in terms of company culture and morale."

And then Mr. Jenkins nodded and smiled really big and gave me a hard high-five.

20

Mr. Jenkins Told Me...

"You Can Take It from Here."

I always assumed Mr. Jenkins would sell the company, cash out, and travel the world with Reneé. It was no secret that the big, national companies all wanted to buy us.

But one morning I woke up and knew that Mr. Jenkins wasn't going to sell the company. He was going to keep it a family-owned business. I don't know how I knew that, but I did.

It turned out that I was right. Later that same day, Mr. Jenkins put me in charge. He still comes in every day and I hope he always will, but on my first day as president of Morris-Jenkins I decided the most important thing I could do was create a little handbook for new employees, telling them exactly what they could expect during their time with us.

My goal, of course, was to communicate all the most important things that Mr. Jenkins told me and to do that in the fewest possible words, which, it turns out, is exactly 2,527.

It seems appropriate that I should wrap up our time together by sharing those 2,527 words with you. But before I do, please let me say how honored I am that you chose to read this little book.

Did you find something in it that you can use to help you reach your goals?

Were you encouraged to learn that the pathway to success isn't a flat highway but an up-and-down walking path through the mountains, just like the path you're walking now?

Here are those 2,527 words I wrote for new employees.

Mr. Jenkins Told Me...
The "Why" Behind Morris-Jenkins

1. Our Management Team Has a Responsibility to You

We don't believe you showed up here by accident.
We believe you're here for a reason.
And if that's true, then we have a responsibility to you,
because that means we're not here by accident either.

At Morris-Jenkins, it's our duty to:

1. provide ethical leadership,

2. be a positive influence, and

3. help you develop and grow.

But you also have a responsibility to us. That responsibility is to grow and develop and become better tomorrow than you are today.

Please understand, we're not looking for perfection. It's ok to do something imperfectly until you've learned to do it well. We're just looking for ongoing improvement.

2. The Role of Culture in a Service Business

We define culture as the values and practices shared by the members of an organization. In simple language, culture is "how we do things around here."

The stronger the culture, the fewer rules and regulations you need. When the culture is strong, you can trust everyone to do the right thing. People can be independent.

Have you ever noticed how families don't require written rules and regulations? That's because there's such a strong trust and culture that it replaces any need for detailed instructions. In companies where the culture is weak, you slow down, refer to the rules and regulations or, even worse, call your manager and ask what to do. The end result is a frustrating experience for the customer.

Here's why culture is so vital at Morris-Jenkins: we're in the business of delivering seven-days-a-week service to our customers' homes. Our Customer Service Representatives are either online or on the phone with our customers every day. We have no control over these real-time conversations. And, once our technicians leave our shop, we have no control over them either.

So how can we be sure our customers receive the service experience we want them to have? Do we give everyone detailed rules and instructions for every situation that could possibly come up?

No... a service business is far too situational to ask employees to stick to inflexible rules and policies. Plus, we know that we're not smart enough to teach every employee how to act in every situation. But we believe you're smart enough to do the right thing if we give you the freedom to do it. And we also believe that you've embraced our culture and want to do what's right.

That's why we asked you to join our team!

So what we do is rely on a strong culture and give you high level principles—guidelines—to help *you* in every situation.

3. Our Purpose and Our Core Values Are Your Guidelines at the Highest Level

Our Purpose: To make it easy for our customers to do business with us.

Our Core Values: To abide by an absolute commitment to honesty, integrity, fairness, and respect for each individual.

Honesty

Being open, trustworthy, and truthful. Refusing to lie, steal, or deceive in any way.

With honesty, you can trust things to be as they appear.

Integrity

Doing the right thing in all circumstances. It includes doing what we say we will do.

Fairness

Treating everyone in an unbiased way in accordance with accepted rules and principles.

It includes the proper balancing of conflicting interests. Example:

- Being fair to the customer
- Being fair to the individual
- Being fair to the team
- Being fair to the company

Respect

Our definition of respect includes two parts:

1. How we feel about someone
2. How we treat him or her

Having respect for someone means we think good things about who a person is, or how that person acts. Showing respect to someone means we act in a way that shows we care about their feelings and well-being.

In summary, we expect that in any given situation, our employees will be honest, behave with integrity, treat others fairly, and show respect to everyone. We also expect our employees to do everything possible to make the service experience easy for our customers.

4. Opportunity Always Comes in the Form of Change

Yesterday doesn't live here anymore. It isn't coming back, and we can't recreate it. Today has already moved in.

Not all that long ago, no company provided air conditioning or plumbing service on the weekend. And if a customer needed a new air conditioner, it wasn't unusual to have to wait days or even weeks to get it installed.

That created a poor customer service experience, and we decided to improve it. So, what happened? Well, we experienced a lot of change when we introduced seven-day-a-week service.

Then we experienced big change when we introduced same-day-installation.

We experienced even more change when we began working 'til midnight.

But our team—people like you—figured out how to do it, because they were determined to make it easy for our customers to do business with us.

We experienced change once again when we added plumbing to our list of services.

But there was our team, figuring out once again how to make it easy for our customers to do business with us.

Every situation presents its own special problems, together with new opportunities. And our special team of people always figures out how to solve those problems and take advantage of the opportunities.

And you're a member of that team.

You're here for a reason.

5. Problems Serve a Purpose

A problem is an opportunity to learn, and that particular problem will be presented to you in various forms until you've learned your lesson. As soon as you've learned what you need to learn from that problem, it goes away.

But you'll get another one.

Why? To give you an opportunity to solve it, and to grow, and to become a larger person.

The purpose of a problem is to teach us, to help us build our muscles, and to grow stronger.

If a person had no problems, they would have no strength.

When you grow as a person, your responsibility grows and the problems presented to you grow in size, as well. The more successful you become at problem-solving, the more you will be advanced. And then even larger problems will be presented to you.

You can measure a person by the size of problems they solve.

We want you to become a giant.
(But a nice giant. Not one of those mean ones.)

6. At Morris-Jenkins, You Will Work with Imperfect People

In the movie *First Knight* starring Sean Connery, King Arthur accepted imperfect people. He chose Lancelot, a man with obvious flaws but also many strengths, to join his select group, the Knights of the Roundtable. He was criticized, and here was his reply: "I can't take my men in pieces...I take them whole...or I take them not at all."

Just as King Arthur couldn't pick and choose the parts of Lancelot he would accept, we don't get to pick and choose the parts of the people we work with, either.

People are quirky and imperfect. We take them whole, or not at all.

Here's the upside: if we accept others as they are, maybe they'll accept us as we are, too. Because none of us is perfect.

But that's great news! Because our beauty is in our imperfections. The "perfect me" is a facade, a mask we wear. And we're never really happy when we're pretending to be someone we're not. And frankly, it's exhausting.

The "real me" is flawed, but it's authentic. We can connect with that person.

We like "the real me."

We like the real you.

And here's some additional encouragement. At Morris-Jenkins we're looking for talent. We don't care what shape, race, color, ethnicity, gender, or sexual orientation it comes in. We're just looking for talent, and we think that we've found it in you.

We're glad that you're here.

7. Conflict Occurs at Intersections

The biggest misconception about conflict is that it's bad. In truth, conflict is neither good nor bad. *How it's managed* determines if it's good or bad.

Conflict is destructive when one side wins at another's expense, or when it destroys morale, polarizes groups, or reduces cooperation.

On the other hand, conflict can be the source of great creativity, excitement, and strength. It can help an organization develop the muscle it needs to succeed and grow. Conflict keeps a company alive—and flourishing—when it stimulates healthy interaction, opens up issues of importance, strengthens team spirit, and results in better solutions to problems.

Whether conflict works for or against an organization depends on only one thing: *how it is managed.*

We don't have room in this booklet to explain all the rules of conflict management. But we do want you to know that we encourage healthy conflict, the kind of conflict where participants are treated with respect, the kind of conflict where each participant is free to fully voice their opinions.

While we also don't have room to fully explain the principles of healthy conflict, we do want to point out where most business conflict occurs. Think about car crashes. Most crashes happen at intersections where one car is going one way and another car is going in a different direction.

So, if most conflict occurs at intersections, what are those intersections in a business? It's simple. Most conflict occurs at the intersections between departments. It's where one department hands off work to another department.

Here's an example: a salesperson sells a new air conditioner and furnace to a customer and sends the paperwork to the Installation Department to be installed. The installation team loads up the equipment, drives to the customer's home, installs the equipment, cleans the job site, and gets ready to leave. The customer then asks, "But where's my new Smart Thermostat?"

The installer goes over the paperwork with a fine-tooth comb. The "Smart Thermostat" isn't mentioned anywhere on the sales proposal. The installer has to drive back to the shop, pick up the thermostat, return to the customer's house, and install it. In total, an extra two hours added to the installer's work day. There's going to be conflict.

Likewise, there will be conflict on the management team during the budgeting process. Does the Installation Department get new trucks this year or does the Service Department?

Always remember: conflict happens when the needs or desires of two or more parties appear incompatible. It is inevitable, at some point, in all personal relationships. Whenever people with individual needs are brought together, there exists the potential for disagreement. But that disagreement should be conducted in a healthy, productive manner.

8. Consequences Drive Behavior

Here's a wake-up call to all managers… Big News!!!

People often don't do what they're told. If they did, they would only eat healthy food, never drink too much alcohol, and exercise regularly.

Even though people don't do what they're told, most businesses are run as if they do. At Morris-Jenkins we don't do that because here's what we know:

The behavior of our employees is critical to the experience our customers receive when they call us and we provide service at their home. We want our employees to be honest, show integrity, treat our customers fairly, and be respectful. We also want them to do everything they can to make the service experience easy. So, you can see that our employees' behavior is very important to us.

We've learned that if we want to influence behavior, there are two ways to do that. We can either do something *before* the behavior occurs or do something *after* the behavior occurs. An action taken before the behavior is called an antecedent. An action taken after the behavior is called a consequence.

Antecedents come before the behavior and set the stage for the behavior to occur. They don't cause the behavior to occur.

Consequences follow the behavior and alter the probability that the behavior will reoccur. They cause the behavior to occur more or less often in the future.

Antecedents have limited control over behavior. It's the role of an antecedent to get a behavior to occur once, or at most a few times. It's the role of a consequence to get it to occur often.

Most businesses invest heavily in antecedent activity such as memos, training, policies, etc. We do too. But the difference is that we understand the limits of what that will do. We understand that training's proper role is to get the behavior to occur once, not to ensure that it is repeated in the future.

For that we need to have a consequence in place, one that will cause the behavior to occur more often in the future. So, we provide reinforcement for that behavior.

Reinforcement can be positive or negative. It can be immediate or in the future. It can be certain or it can be uncertain.

We've found that the most powerful reinforcement is positive, immediate, and certain.

Positive + Immediate + Certain = Powerful

That's why we believe that both praise and correction should be immediate. But praise should be public. Correction should be private.

The culture of Morris-Jenkins is one of praise and public recognition.

It is positive. It is immediate. It is certain.

9. Complexity is the Enemy

Left to itself, an organization will become complex. There is constant pressure to create detailed rules and regulations. But if we let that happen, success will be defined and measured by adherence to those rules and regulations, instead of being measured by what's truly important.

We must fight complexity with everything we've got.

Our success is defined by:

1. taking care of our customers,
2. growing our revenues, and
3. controlling expenses.

We keep things simple. But simple is never easy.

Here's an example: there are a lot of factors that affect the success of a business.

But only four or five of those things make 80% of the difference.

So we focus on those things.

If you help us execute those four or five things, we will be wildly successful.

Thanks for your help!

We knew we could count on you.

10. Celebrate Everything... Celebrate, Celebrate, Celebrate!

You're going to enjoy attending the meetings at Morris-Jenkins. If you didn't enjoy the meetings where you've worked in the past, then they weren't doing it right.

The purpose of meetings at Morris-Jenkins is three-fold:

1. **To keep you informed about what's going on.**

   We believe every member of the team deserves to know what's happening.

2. **To share new skills, new insights, and new perspectives.**

   You will leave every meeting stronger and better than you arrived.

3. **To give praise and public recognition.**

   When we get a happy call from a customer or a really positive online review, we read those with pride during our meetings and recognize the people who made those customers happy. And we celebrate!

We don't just celebrate the touchdowns, we celebrate the first downs.

Celebration is praise taken to its highest level.
That's why celebration is our highest tradition.
Can we count on you to celebrate with us?
We can? Excellent!
We knew we were going to like you.

\# \# \# \#